TRANSPORTATION
FROM THEN TO NOW

transportation

noun

1. an act, process, or instance of transporting or being transported

2. a. means of conveyance or travel from one place to another
   b. public conveyance of passengers or goods especially as a commercial enterprise

Carol Lawrence

illustrated by
Ran Zheng

Albert Whitman & Company
Chicago, Illinois

For Mona, Belle, Magic, and Petal, with thanks—CL

To my parents for supporting me on all my journeys—RZ

Library of Congress Cataloging-in-Publication data is on file with the publisher.
Text copyright © 2021 by Carol Lawrence
Illustrations copyright © 2021 by Albert Whitman & Company
Illustrations by Ran Zheng
First published in the United States of America in 2021
by Albert Whitman & Company

ISBN 978-0-8075-8059-2 (hardcover)
ISBN 978-0-8075-8058-5 (ebook)

Printed in China

10 9 8 7 6 5 4 3 2 1 WKT 24 23 22 21 20

Design by Rick DeMonico

For more information about Albert Whitman & Company,
visit our website at www.albertwhitman.com.

Transportation helps us communicate, it helps us make and move goods across the United States and overseas, and it allows people to move around the world. By doing these things, it helps us develop and grow local and worldwide communities. It helps develop civilization. Transportation is critical to the ways we live.

But people have also shaped transportation. We've always built and used the transportation we need. People near water built boats; people in deserts used camels. And everywhere, everyone walked. Today, people move around easily, by rail, road, sea, or air. Our lifestyles—the way we live—have helped create transportation just as much as transportation has helped shape how we live.

Our earliest form of transportation was our feet. Humans walked to get from place to place.

Then came the boat. The oldest known boat is a dugout, similar to a canoe, and made from a hollowed-out tree trunk. It dates back to 8000 BCE and is now in a museum in the Netherlands, the country where it was found.

From the moment the wheel was first used in about 3500 BCE, it signaled a big change. About three hundred years later, someone put wooden wheels on a chariot. The wheelbarrow was the first time the wheel was used to transport goods. The wheel meant we could move things. It really did set everything in motion.

The first wheel was a potter's wheel, in Mesopotamia in about 3500 BCE.

The wheelbarrow made life easier, it saved people time, and that meant it saved money too.

The wheelbarrow may have been invented in Greece or in China—no one knows for sure—anywhere from 500 BCE to 100 BCE, and it showed up again in medieval Europe.

At almost the same time that the wheel was first used, in about 3000 BCE, people in the Middle East started riding donkeys along a trade route through the foothills of central Israel to Palestine. Horses then replaced the donkey, both for people to ride and to carry goods.

Although Paleolithic people drew pictures of horses on cave walls as early as 30,000 BCE, horses weren't tamed and ridden until about 3000 BCE, by the Botai. They were nomadic hunter-gatherers living on the Eurasian steppe, stretching from Hungary to China.

The first chariots were built between 3000 BCE and 2000 BCE in Mesopotamia. Soldiers used chariots pulled by horses as moving platforms in battle. People rode in chariots before riding horseback, maybe because horses weren't strong enough until people domesticated them and bred them for strength. Historians believe that civilization as we know it began in Mesopotamia, and that these advances contributed to its beginning.

Chariots were heavy with solid wooden wheels and frames.

After donkeys and horses, people rode dromedary camels with one hump, sometime between 3000 BCE and 900 BCE in Arabia, a peninsula of western Asia, northeast of Africa. The Bactrian camel, with two humps, was tamed sometime between 4000 BCE to 2500 BCE in the steppes of Central Asia, cold and dry grasslands that stretch about 5,000 miles from Hungary to Manchuria in northeast Asia.

Because camels can walk long distances without water, they were well suited to the places where they were ridden.

In about 3100 BCE, Ancient Egypt was prosperous, partly because of its position on the lower Nile River in North Africa. The Egyptians may have invented sailboats to move goods on the river. The first boats were bundles of papyrus, reeds that grew along the marshes, tied together.

The first sails were large squares of papyrus. The boats could only sail in the direction the wind pushed them.

When a boat needed to go into the wind, people rowed.

In about 3000 BCE, the Egyptians made the first wood-planked boats, called Abydos boats, named after the city where they were discovered in 1991. Woven straps were tied together into long planks, or wooden pegs joined the planks together. Reeds or grass were stuffed between the planks to help seal them. Abydos boats were about 75 feet long. They were probably steered by one oar and were used for trade with other cities.

A large, full-sized ship, 143 feet long, was found in 1954 in a pit at the foot of the Great Pyramid of Giza.

During the Roman Empire, which lasted from 27 BCE to 476 CE, the Romans built more than 53,000 miles of roads, which they used to transport goods and people, including their armies and supplies.

Pedestrians could walk on footpaths, sometimes paved, on both sides of the roads, with seats for resting.

The Romans traveled by foot, on carts, in chariots, and on boats. Travel by boat was more comfortable than by road because the carts, wagons, and chariots didn't have springs, and bounced. In Rome, streets were narrow and busy. A wealthy person was often carried by litter, a seat between two long poles, on which people could lie back a little, or by sedan chair, on which they sat upright. Both litters and sedan chairs were covered and had curtains for privacy.

The Romans also built bridges over rivers.

Native tribes in North America lived in different regions and used different kinds of transport.

If the tribes were near water, they used dugouts and also bark canoes.

Bark canoes were in two parts: a wooden frame and an outer shell of bark, usually birch, that was in one piece and stretched over the frame.

Some Plains tribes used sleds and toboggans.

The sleds had two runners of wood or leather on either side of a wooden body; sleds were pulled by people or by dogs, which were used before horses.

The toboggans were like sleds but didn't have runners; they had flat bottoms with curved fronts.

Some people also used kayaks or umiaks.

An umiak was an open boat made of animal skin stretched over a wooden frame.

The kayak was similar, but it wasn't open.

Native people who lived where it snowed used snowshoes. There were many different kinds, depending on how deep the snow was in a region.

The Plains tribes also used a wooden sled called a travois, which had two long wooden poles, crossed at one end. That end was put across the shoulders of the animal pulling the sled, so the poles wouldn't fall off.

When the first European settlers came to North America, they traveled by land or by sea. Either way was difficult, expensive, and dangerous, so most people didn't go far from home—a big difference from later travel. Poor settlers and enslaved people walked. Women stayed home and took care of the house and children.

Men walked very long distances, usually for supplies or to visit family and friends. In the South, colonists bought horses as soon as they could afford them. Horseback riding was mainly used for transportation, but men also enjoyed riding on their estates.

If they could afford it, farmers purchased carts to help transport goods, or wagons to use on their farms and also to take their goods to town, to sell or trade.

The Conestoga wagon was the earliest kind of the American covered wagon, used in the late 1700s and in the 1800s. Its floor curved upward to stop the goods it carried from moving around, and its sides were canvas.

The Conestoga wagon could carry a lot of goods, about six tons, over long distances. It was pulled by horses, mules, or oxen.

Travel by sea in the 1700s and 1800s had advanced since the Mayflower carried the first English Pilgrims to what they called the New World in 1620, but journeys across the Atlantic Ocean still took six to eight weeks, maybe more, depending on the weather.

Ships were also used to carry enslaved people from Africa to the United States between 1518 and the early 1800s. The ships were overcrowded and conditions were terrible, but the people were forced to travel.

Journeys were dangerous and difficult, taking a long time, even along American coasts. There could be shipwrecks, illness, and pirates.

Boats were used in the American Revolution, from 1775 to 1783. The American colonies had no naval force in the war, and their ships were greatly outnumbered by the British. But the colonials had privately owned armed ships that were paid to fight the British. This was an important part of the revolution for the colonials.

The American clippers, built for speed, set sail in the 1800s and were used commonly until the 1900s. The clippers were so fast that they changed worldwide trade. In 1851, a ship called *Flying Cloud* sailed from New York to San Francisco in eighty-nine days and twenty-one hours, a speed record that remained unbeaten until 1989. The clipper ships' popularity faded when railroads were built across North America in the 1870s, and when steamships began sailing across the Atlantic in the late 1800s.

Clipper ships had a big impact on the social history of America. The men who owned them grew rich and put their money into coal, railroads, mining, real estate, and the transatlantic cable under the sea, which allowed financial information to be communicated almost immediately from Europe to America.

Many kinds of land transportation that changed people's lives and our society were invented in the late 1700s, and continue to be used to this day.

In 1769, Nicolas-Joseph Cugnot, a Frenchman, invented the first self-propelled mechanical land vehicle; basically, the world's first real automobile.

Cugnot's invention was like a large, heavy, steam-powered tricycle. It was unstable and the boiler had to be relit every fifteen minutes but it worked.

In 1783, the French Montgolfier brothers invented the first hot-air balloon. The first piloted flight held a local physics and chemistry teacher.

In 1817, a German named Baron Karl von Drais invented the bicycle. It didn't have pedals, so the rider had to run to keep it moving. A Scottish blacksmith, Kirkpatrick Macmillan, may have invented the first pedal bicycle in 1839, made of wood. But several French inventors may have invented it in the 1860s, with pedals attached to the front wheel.

In 1804, the first steam locomotive was invented by Richard Trevithick, a British inventor and mining engineer. It ran along a track in Wales.

The Scotsman James Watt had already pioneered the steam engine, but Trevithick's version used steam at a very high pressure, which meant it could be used in different types of transportation, including ships and locomotives, as well as in mines, on farms, and in factories. Trevithick contributed to the change in society, not only because of his invention but also because of when it happened, during the First Industrial Revolution from the mid-1700s to the mid-1800s.

Trevithick's locomotive pulled five cars loaded with iron and ironworkers about nine miles. It was so heavy that it broke the rails it ran on after just a few trips.

The First Industrial Revolution arose mainly in Britain, from the mid-1700s to about 1830. From the mid-1800s to the early 1900s, it spread to Europe and the United States, when it was called the Second Industrial Revolution. Textile manufacturing moved from homes to factories. Large factories began to mass-produce goods. Steam power helped this to happen, and it changed our world. People followed jobs from rural areas to cities.

Transportation changed from feet, horses, and sailboats to railroads, steamboats, and automobiles. This changed the way people traveled and the way goods were shipped around the world, forever.

The Baltimore and Ohio Railroad was the first railway in the United States to carry commercial passengers and goods. The railway's first section opened in 1830, and the first cars were pulled by horses. The one-way route was 1.5 miles, and a ticket cost nine cents. The line was later powered by steam and extended into Virginia. By the time of the United States Civil War in 1861, it was an important route for the Union states. After the war, the line was extended into Ohio, Indiana, Illinois, Missouri, Pennsylvania, New York, Ohio, and West Virginia.

The first transcontinental railroad was completed in 1869 when the Central Pacific and the Union Pacific lines were joined. This coast-to-coast railroad changed the settlement and the economy of the West completely. Passengers and goods were now transported quickly, safely, and less expensively.

Although people moving west still traveled by wagon, trains became faster and more frequent, allowing settlements to grow quickly. Train travel dominated, and changed society.

Trains were very important to a changing American landscape, but the first gas engine automobile in 1860 brought even greater change. Étienne Lenoir, a Belgian engineer, developed the first internal combustion engine, which used coal gas and air to create energy that, through a series of mechanisms, turned a vehicle's wheels. He put it into a frame and created the first gas engine automobile.

In 1885, the first usable, practical automobile, as we know it, was built by Karl Benz, a German engineer.

Benz's automobile had two seats, a compact internal combustion engine at the rear, a tubular steel frame, and three wire-spoked wheels.

In 1888, without his knowledge, Benz's wife, Bertha, drove the car with their two sons, for about 112 miles, proving its usefulness.

Also in Germany in 1885, Gottlieb Daimler and Wilhelm Maybach invented the modern motorcycle, attaching a small, petroleum-based combustion engine to a wooden bicycle frame. It was called the Daimler Reitwagen.

In the United States, Henry Ford produced his Model T automobile from 1908 to 1927. The car was practical, and it was an affordable means of transportation for many people, not just for the wealthy. Henry Ford kept costs down by manufacturing the cars on an assembly line rather than building the cars one at a time. The Model T raised people's standard of living and was the beginning of people's love of cars.

The Model T was basic but it was faster than a horse and it could go farther.

People had to start the Model T by turning a crank handle. The car began to move forward slowly, as soon as it started, so people had to move quickly, from the front where the crank was, to get into the car. The crank led to many broken arms.

Henry Ford's Model T was so popular that the government had to build roads for the cars.

Cars revolutionized transportation. They gave Americans personal freedom, transforming our society, shaping our nation and our culture, and they did this quickly. The growing middle class, mostly living in the suburbs after World War II, saw the car as a necessity. It helped people commute to cities, giving them the transportation that suburbs didn't have.

The Wright brothers took the Montgolfier brothers'
venture into the air one giant step further in 1903,
when they succeeded, after many attempts, in getting
their Wright flyer to fly not once but four times in one
day. That basic design of the first airplane the brothers
invented, built, and flew at Kitty Hawk, North Carolina,
led to air travel as we know it today.

Airplanes need four things to fly: lift, weight, thrust, and drag. Lift comes from the difference in air pressure between the air that flows over a wing's curved top and its flat bottom. The pressure of air on the bottom is greater than the pressure on the top, and this pushes the plane up.

Planes are designed so that air is guided smoothly to the side, which reduces drag. A plane goes up if the lift and thrust are greater than the weight and the drag.

The weight is the force of gravity that pulls the plane down to Earth. The thrust comes from the engines. Smaller planes have propellers; large planes have jet engines. Jet engines shoot exhaust gases out from the back, which moves the plane forward. Drag slows the plane down; it's the force of the air against the plane as it moves forward.

We now had transportation by sea with ships, by land with the railroad and the car, and by air.

What came next were rockets, in 1942, when Germany launched a ballistic missile off the Baltic coast. It was the first rocket capable of reaching space.

Ballistic Missile

Sputnik

The first rocket that launched something into space was built by the Soviet Union. It launched Sputnik, the first satellite, in 1957.

The Soviet Union and the United States were in a space race, sending dogs and monkeys into space, before the Soviets sent the first man, Yuri Gagarin, into Earth's orbit in 1961. In 1962, John Glenn became the first American to orbit Earth. In 1969, the first moon-landing mission, by Apollo 11's lunar module, was a success.

Since 1971, there have been space stations that orbit Earth for long periods of time. They are research laboratories, with crews conducting experiments.

Millions of people watched astronaut Neil Armstrong take that "giant leap for mankind," followed by Buzz Aldrin, while Michael Collins stayed in orbit around the moon.

The first space shuttle, *Columbia*, was launched in 1981. The shuttle let people fly in the same spacecraft into space more than once.

Since then, rockets have been used to send spacecraft farther and farther into our solar system, past the moon, to other planets and their moons.

In 2012, *Voyager I* left our solar system and reached interstellar space.

Voyager I

Now, there are private individuals and companies who are selling space travel to the moon, for people who can afford the cost of a ticket. NASA also wants to send astronauts back to the moon.

As people invented new kinds of transportation, from carts, to wagons, to boats, to railroads, to cars, each type changed the way we lived. And each allowed people to travel farther from where they were born, making the world interconnected economically through trade, ideas, and culture. We may continue to invent new ways to travel, reaching even further into space, changing our lives even more.

Author's Note

Transportation has been one of the most important elements in civilization. It has not only helped people move from place to place; it has also helped us to communicate. Before the creation of personal phones and tablets, laptops and computers, people relied on landline telephones, and post offices around the world to stay in touch. That was how friends, families, companies, schools, medical organizations, governments—all critical to society—were able to help one another by sharing information.

Transportation has helped shape our expanding world, through travel across the globe and, more recently, through trips into space. And people have helped shape transport, by inventing the kinds of transportation to fill society's needs, making travel by rail, road, sea, and air easier.

We don't know for sure when some kinds of transport we take for granted today were first used, or even who invented them, so there are different possibilities included in this book. But no matter who invented something or when it was first used, everything led us to where we are today. The development and advancement of transportation itself transformed our world.

Although many people have stopped traveling or are traveling less now, transportation is still as important to us now as it has always been, and as it always will be.

Glossary

ballistic missile: a powered missile with a high, arching curve.

Civil War: in the United States this is also called the War between the States, which took place from 1861–1865.

galaxy: a system of millions or billions of stars together with gas and dust held together by gravity.

gravity: on Earth, the force that pulls down toward the planet's center.

interstellar space: what exists between star systems in a galaxy.

medieval Europe: also called the Middle Ages; the period between the fall of the Roman Empire in 476 BCE and the beginning of the fourteenth century.

Mesopotamia: an historical part of Asia between the Tigris and Euphrates rivers that flow through what is now Iraq.

Paleolithic: relating to the Old Stone Age, when the first rough tools, made of rock, stone, bone, and wood were used.

satellite: a man-made object put into orbit around Earth or another planet to gather information.

solar system: the sun and everything that travels around it.

space shuttle: a spacecraft with people on board, launched by a rocket and able to land, used to make repeated trips.

space stations: large satellites used as a long-term base for people who go into space.

star system: a large number of stars with a structure; also called a galaxy.

World War I: the war from 1914–1918 in which countries around the world chose sides and fought one another.

World War II: the war from 1939–1945 in which countries around the world chose sides and fought one another.